Love
Is the Answer

Blythe Ayne, Ph.D.

BOOKS & AUDIO BY BLYTHE AYNE, PH.D.

Nonfiction:
Love Is The Answer
45 Ways To Excellent Life
Finding Your Path, Engaging Your Purpose
Horn of Plenty — The Cornucopia of Your Life

How to Save Your Life Series:
Save Your Life With The Power Of pH Balance
Save Your Life With The Phenomenal Lemon
Save Your Life with Stupendous Spices
Save Your Life with the Elixir of Water

Absolute Beginner Series:
Bed Yoga – Easy, Healing, Yoga Moves You Can Do in Bed
Write Your Book! Publish Your Book! Market Your Book!

Fiction:
The Darling Undesirables Series:
The Heart of Leo - short story prequel
The Darling Undesirables
Moons Rising
The Inventor's Clone
Heart's Quest

Novellas & Short Story Collections:
5 Minute Stories
Lovely Frights for Lonely Nights
When Fields Hum & Glow

Children's Illustrated Books:
The Rat Who Didn't Like Rats
The Rat Who Didn't Like Christmas

Poetry, Photography & Art:
Life Flows on the River of Love
Home & the Surrounding Territory

Audio:
Thr Power of pH Balance–Dr. Blythe Ayne Interviews Steven Acuff

Blythe Ayne's paperback books, hardbound books, & ebooks
can be purchased wherever books are sold.

Love Is the Answer

Blythe Ayne, Ph.D.

Love is the Answer
Blythe Ayne, Ph.D.

Emerson & Tilman, Publishers
129 Pendleton Way #55
Washougal, WA 98671

All Rights Reserved
No part of this publication may be reproduced, distributed, or transmitted in any form, or by any means, including photocopying, recording, or other electronic or mechanical methods, without the prior written permission of the author, except brief quotations in critical reviews and other noncommercial uses permitted by copyright law.

All graphics © by Blythe Ayne

www.BlytheAyne.com
Blythe@BlytheAyne.com

Love is the Answer

Excellent Life Series - Book 4

ebook ISBN: 978-1-947151-02-4
Paperback ISBN: 978-1-947151-00-0
Hardbound ISBN: 978-1-947151-01-7

[BODY, MIND & SPIRIT / Inspiration & Personal Growth
BODY, MIND & SPIRIT / Mindfulness & Meditation
BODY, MIND & SPIRIT / Healing / Prayer & Spiritual]

BIC: FM

DEDICATION

– For My Parents –

*The first to teach me
About the Power and Comfort of Love
With Gratitude, Respect, Appreciation,
But Most of All,
Love*

Love is the Answer

Table of Contents:

1	The Light of Love	3
2	Exponential Increase	5
3	Love Loves Love	7
4	Answering Love	9
5	The Greatest Lesson	11
6	Eternity's Pocket	13
7	The Greatest Force	17
8	Hunger for Love	19
9	In The Moment	21
10	The Force of Love	23
11	Mosquito Love	25
12	Love Never Fails	29
13	The Single Power	33
14	Self Love	35
15	Arriving Where You Are	37
16	Out-Reasoning Reason	39
17	Love at the Core	41
18	Love Performs the Impossible	43
19	Unite in Love	47
20	Love Likes Everybody	49
21	More Love, Less Paperwork	51

22	Love Inspires	53
23	The Circle of Love	55
24	Truth & Love	57
25	Love Prevails	59
26	Faith, Hope, Love	61
27	Love's Home	63
28	Honey Love	65
29	Only Believe in Love	67
30	Love's Miracles	69
31	Compassion	71
32	Compassion for Oneself	75
33	Aura	79
34	The Gates of Heaven	81
35	The Flower of Love	83
36	Love Heals All	85
37	The Spirit of Love	87
38	Love's True Means	89
39	Timeless Love	93
40	Real Love Stories	95
41	Daring to Love	99
42	Money Can't Buy Me Love	101
43	Love's Instinct	103
44	The Best in Others	105
45	The Warp & Woof of Love	107
46	Love Conquers All	109
47	Listen for Love's Voice	111

48	Love's Tenacity	113
49	Amazing Love	115
50	Love Is All There Is	119

Images:

Two Oars and a Birdhouse	2
Swainson's Thrush Nest with Babies	6
Second Cousin's Wedding	15
Parent's 50th Wedding Anniversary	16
Water Wheel – Bothell, Washington	28
Keeping Cupid Prisoner	32
Lori, Ben and Little Lori	47
Gazing Ball	56
Taj Mahal	62
In the Secret Garden	66
Nyxie – "I Miss You"	74
Mother and Little Lori	78
Dove House	82
Two Moths	92
Blarney Castle	98
Tree Growing Out of Ancient Step Pyramid	112
Two Goslings	118
Dear Reader	119
About the Author	120

Thank you to T. L. Trevaskis and Brenda Jones for their expert proofreading.

All images © Blythe Ayne

1

THE LIGHT OF LOVE

Without becoming intimately acquainted with the pilot light of love burning at one's center, the furnace of full engagement in life cannot be ignited. What pleasures ceaselessly abound in the light and warmth of love!

Where awe resides, which is a state of active love overtaking your every molecule, the very blades of grass reveal their pulsating glow of life in the night, the deer comes up to you and touches your ear as you sit on the grass in resplendent meditation.

The wounded human heart becomes whole as you pass the torch of love.

Your own problems, which seemed so insurmountable, become small and fade away. All in the warmth and the power of love.

> *"Love must be as much a light as it is a flame."*
> **Henry David Thoreau**

2
EXPONENTIAL INCREASE

Love has a very interesting action—the more it is given away, the more it becomes. The cup of love poured out becomes a bucket, the bucket spills over into a stream, the stream flows into a river, the river fills the oceans—that is the energy of love.

> *"The love we give away*
> *is the only love we keep."*
> **Elbert Hubbard**

3

LOVE LOVES LOVE

The only thing stubborn about love is its belief in itself. When everything seems a muddle and the clouds appear very dark indeed, love always breaks through and shows us the way.

We can choose to be sleeping or say we are blind, we can say there is no love, or it's not to be found, but love is always and ever right here, making us whole by touching our soul, and uniting us to the Force of Life.

We cannot cut the thread connecting us to our creating source—while, at the same time, love does not force itself upon us.

> *"If you have love in your life it makes up for a great many things you lack. If you don't have love, no matter what else there is, it's not enough."*
> ***Ann Landers***

4

ANSWERING LOVE

At the door of your being is a patient, tender, knock, not a huge, booming, "let me in or else" knock. We make our choice to answer or not answer this knock. The purpose of life is to have our experiences by the path of our choices. We're never forced to unite with love. But our wisdom teaches us that "love is the way."

There are many other seeming paths. Yet all of those paths are painful and rocky and blocked, if not manifested of love. They are illusions, while the light of love glows behind every illusory boulder and under every phantom pebble, encouraging us—only look upon love to see the open path that was always there.

> *"Behold, I stand at the door and knock."*
> ***Revelation 3:20***

5

THE GREATEST LESSON

Love is patient. Love waits, and is content to wait, for twenty-two months for a baby elephant to make its trunk and tail and all that's between before coming into this world.

Love waits, and is content to wait, for Winter to become Spring, Spring to become Summer, Summer to become Autumn and Autumn to become Winter again.

Love waits, and is patient to wait, while we learn the Golden Rule, which resides in sympathy—"I understand how you are like me, and I care about you—and I will treat you as I would like to be treated myself."

Love waits, and is patient to wait, while we discover the step beyond the Golden Rule, to the Platinum Rule which springs from empathy—"I understand how you are not like me, and I care about you – and I will treat you as *you* would desire to be treated."

This is the way to peace, happiness and, yes, the way back to love again.

> *"The greatest thing you'll ever learn*
> *is just to love and to be loved in return."*
> ***Eden Ahbez***

6

ETERNITY'S POCKET

Choose love in every moment. Nothing can go wrong, even when things are going wrong, as long as love is being chosen every moment.

Buddhist teachings revolve around the impermanence of everything. A delightful experience will pass, a painful experience will pass.

The only thing that we can put in our spiritual pocket and take with us into eternity is the love we felt, experienced, and created while going through this life of impermanence.

> *"Love is a choice you make from moment to moment."*
> **Barbara De Angelis**

7

THE GREATEST FORCE

"Where there is great love, there are always miracles."
Willa Cather

There is no greater force, presence, understanding, knowing, or power on earth than love.

Love takes on so many forms as to be seemingly invisible. Yet it is everywhere.

Is there anywhere we can look and not see the overflowing force of love? Not only in glorious sunsets and starry skies, but in a weed, a gnat, a clod of dirt—all pulsing with unconditional love.

If the creative force is God, and God is love, then every single thing that is, has its being in *love*.

> *"God IS Love."*
> **I John 4:8**

8

HUNGER FOR LOVE

A life without love is a life of void. Not that there is such a thing as a life without love in actuality, as we are made of the Stuff of Love.

But if one chooses not to see it, then everything life presents tends to feel hollow and unfulfilling.

There will always be a hunger and a waiting for the Whole Moment, for the true feeling, for the sensation and experience of love.

> *"The hunger for love*
> *is much more difficult to remove*
> *than the hunger for bread."*
> **Mother Teresa**

9

IN THE MOMENT

Be In The Moment.
We are not "alive" in the past, we are not "alive" in the future. The only place we are alive is in this Moment.

The only way to really reside in the gift of the present is to be within the protective, eternal, glowing presence of love.

Whenever we find ourselves woefully in the past or anxiously in the future, come back to the healing balm of This Moment, brought to you by the power and energy, centering and calmness, of love.

> *When you no longer perceive*
> *the world as hostile,*
> *there is no more fear,*
> *and when there is no more fear*
> *Love and compassion arise,*
> *and change the world."*
> **Eckhart Tolle**

10

THE FORCE OF LOVE

What is this otherwise strange life about if not about a force so amazing, so profound, so grand, as to create the virtually invisible quark, and the unfathomably gigantic of the most gigantic stars, to create a human child with the light of the Creator's other dimensions still in her eyes.

What is this life about, if not about a Force of Love? Within ourselves, when our heart spills over, when all our senses—our sight, hearing, smell, taste, touch, thinking and feeling rise to a level that unites all of these senses into one crescendo of enlightenment—that is but the tiniest spark of the energy being created in the image of our Creator, because from that Force of Love did creation manifest.

> *"God's residence is next to mine,*
> *God's furniture is love."*
> **Emily Dickinson**

11

MOSQUITO LOVE

There is nothing that can storm the gates of unconditional love. Unconditional love loves no matter what. It loves the criminal and the innocent. It loves the butterfly and the mosquito.

I recently read an essay where the author was expounding on the wonders of all of creation, but stating that he believed there was one exception, and that exception was the mosquito.

And yet, if ever there was a meaningful creation, it is the mosquito. It teaches us two of our very most important lessons, should we choose to work on those lessons.

One is patience, and the other is unconditional love. That doesn't mean that we need to welcome the mosquito nibbling upon ourselves, but it does mean that much would be easier in this world if we became united in loving all living things unconditionally, if only from the sense of wonder at its existence in the first place.

What kind of love, focus, creativity, and attention would it take to imagine, and then manifest, a mosquito? *Ah!* Even the mosquito invokes our awe if we but stop and contemplate what we're looking at.

And how do we stop and see what we're looking at? By inviting love, unconditional love, to take our minds and hearts to that place where a mosquito could be imagined, and the Creator might have said, "hmmm, these people I brought into being need to find their patience and love.

"I created them in my Image, to create, and yet they cannot manifest their truest and highest calling when they are filled with hate, fear, anger, greed, and mistrust.

"They need a perfect experience of their own unconditional love. Go, therefore, little mosquito, and teach them the greatest lessons!"

> *"Your task is not to seek love,*
> *but merely to seek and find*
> *all the barriers within yourself*
> *that you have built against love."*
> **Rumi**

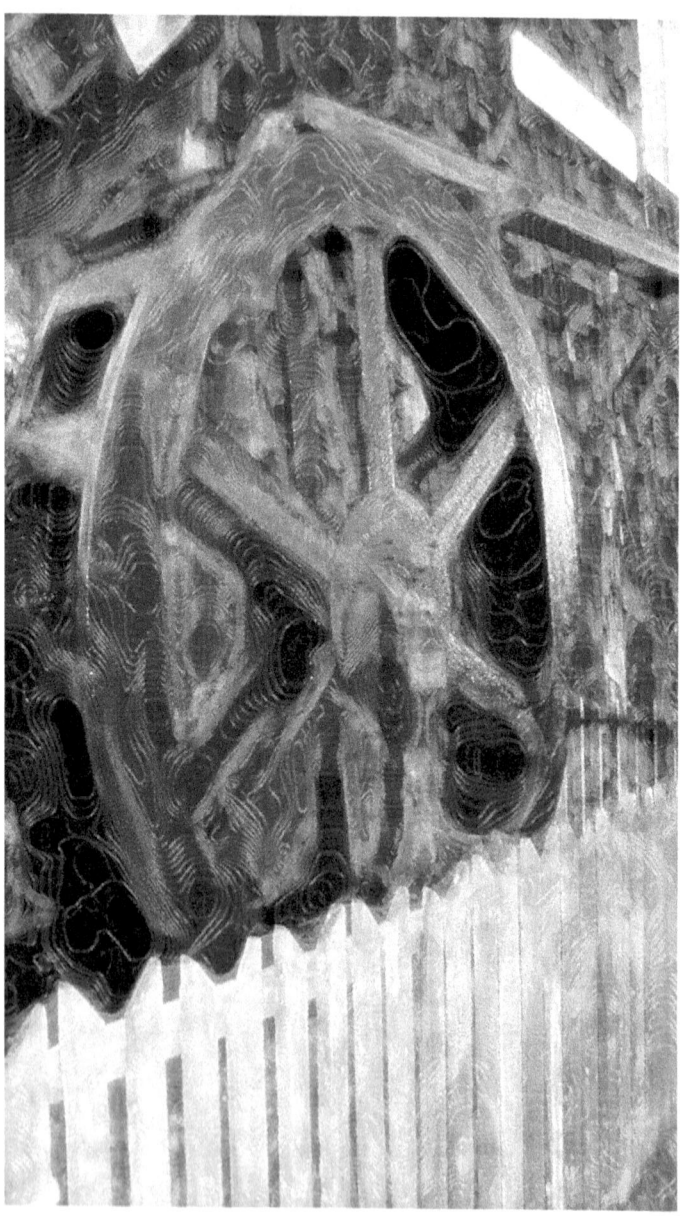

12

LOVE NEVER FAILS

Love is Kind.
Love wishes the very best for every
Creature and Being.
Love does not desire for itself that which
Belongs to another.
Love supports the self-image,
And expands the Joy of every sentient creature.
Love, in general, is modest,

But has a glorious-sounding trumpet
When the sweet fanfares of love are called for.
Love does not get angry when cut off in traffic
Or the grocery line,
It matters not to love to say, "me first."
Love relinquishes hurts done to it
Before the hurt can harm,
Therefore, love does not become a victim.
Love loves the self with the same guileless respect
As love loves others, and
Love loves others with the same
Guileless respect as the self.
Love dwells in goodness and truth.
Love is faithful, believing, knowing,
And ever-present.
Love never fails.

*Love is patient,
love is kind.
It does not envy,
it does not boast,
it is not proud.
It is not rude,
it is not self-seeking.
It is not easily angered,
it keeps no record of wrongs.
Love does not delight in evil,
but rejoices with the truth.
It always protects,
always trusts,
always hopes,
always perseveres.
Love never fails.*

I Corinthians 13:4-8

13

THE SINGLE POWER

Love brings us face to face, and open-heartedly, to our truest truth, our most real reality—those things which motivate us and that call to us from deep within.

Love inspires us to wake up in the morning and allows us to calmly fall into sleep at night. In the cradle of love, we find our peace and our inspiration. Love is happiest when engaged in meaningful action that unites our doing with our being.

If we are not upon the business of our purpose, which is driven by the energy of love, there follows a sense of discomfort. It is easier to get at the tasks and the business of our purpose than to dally or argue with it.

Love is a pervasive, quiet reminder that, although we may wish not to be asked to do anything, we have come into this life with things to do.

Of course, we can choose not to do them! But is it worth the frustration, non-fulfillment, and discontent?

> *"You know quite well, deep within you, that there is only ... a single power... and that is called loving."*
> ***Hermann Hesse***

14

SELF LOVE

What do we all want from life? To be happy.

What do we hope to gain in our daily interactions and endeavors? A sense of reasonable, personal power.

Poor self-esteem is crippling when we feel powerless and unworthy of self-assertion.

Here is the formula to feel your personal power and infinite worthiness:

Love Thyself

Every day, say quietly to yourself, "I love you," or "I love me," or "I love myself."

Pause for a moment and really feel the sensation of love for yourself.

If you find this difficult (a lot of people do) bring to mind a person or a pet until you feel the wonderful sensations of love, issuing out from your solar plexus, that real, true emotion and accompanying bodily feelings, (picture your child, your beloved kitty, your devoted dog) and then insert yourself right into that feeling.

Don't think it, feel it.

> *"If only you would love enough,*
> *you would be the happiest and*
> *most powerful being in the world."*
> **Emmet Fox**

15

ARRIVING WHERE YOU ARE

If one feels that the things one does are out of duty, commitment, obligation or entrapment—remember … remember … how did you arrive here? What was the first step on the path? Because almost certainly it had somewhere within it the seeds of love.

The more we are willing to say this is so, the more rapidly we return to the loving care of love. Then we can recall the steps taken to arrive at a destination away from love and change our understanding of that journey. We can now see the choices we made, and how those choices brought us to this place. We can choose to love ourselves, our path and our present location, which was all that the journey was ever about.

Get back to your place of love, you can arrive there in your mind in a moment. Then wrap it up like a precious, shining jewel and return it to your present life. Bring all that you are and all that you do back to the realm of love.

> *"Love doesn't make the world go 'round;*
> *Love is what makes the ride worthwhile."*
> **Franklin P. Jones**

16

OUT-REASONING REASON

Have you ever been compelled to do something that, when others asked you what the fascination was, (or even, perhaps, when you asked yourself) you could hardly provide an answer?

But still, you were driven to create something, or to do something that would not benefit you, but perhaps benefit another. Did you wonder at yourself for the strength of this urge, when there was little, if any, practical outcome for yourself?

This is the drive of love. Love longs to manifest. It will move us to actions that exceed our uncomplicated, three-dimensional understanding of life. Love comes from the eternal, resides in the eternal and returns to the eternal, about which our comprehension is, at best, imperfect. Sometimes this drive exceeds our reason. But it is undoubtedly the most authentic drive we can be driven by.

> *"The heart has its reasons*
> *which reason knows not of."*
> **Blaise Pascal**

17

LOVE AT THE CORE

Keep love at the core of all actions, thoughts, motivations, intentions, drives, inspirations and creations.

In this way, the partial realizations, shadows, half dreams, faint wishes and broken longings of them will disappear in the bright light of love.

They can come forth, true renditions of themselves, whole and complete.

Do not judge what you are called to do.

Wholeness (Holiness) is always present when you leave all to love.

Leave all for love...
Heartily know...
The gods arrive...
When half-gods go."
Ralph Waldo Emerson

18

LOVE PERFORMS THE IMPOSSIBLE

There is nothing that love cannot do. Love bears hours of labor, bringing a Being from the other side, through the womb—that in-between dimension—to the world of three dimensions.

Love lifts cars off people in an accident. Love rushes into burning buildings to rescue a child, or a dog or a cat. Love throws a rope to people caught in floods and pulls them up to safety. Love plunges headlong into the darkness of mine shafts to pull out air-starved, injured workers. Love leaps up from a meal or sound sleep and rushes to care for those in need, sirens calling.

Love pulls over to the side of the road when the rescue vehicles approach to allow them swift passage. Love whispers a prayer for the person in need as the siren passes.

Love listens patiently, compassionately, to another's sad tale, allowing the sadness to dissipate and disappear.

Love sheds a tear in a touching moment of a silly TV sitcom, or a greeting card ad.

Love understands forgiveness, and forgives seventy times seventy thousand, without becoming a victim.

Love never victimizes.

Love dreams of flying and imagines such machines as can fly. Love travels around and around the globe, making friends of strangers. Love shares its secrets, insinuating love where there is fear, planting love where there is hate, nurturing love where there is mistrust.

Love is the mortar between the individual stones of people, tribes, cultures. Love makes the building and holds it up, when we unite in the open wonderment and awe of our differences, our similarities.

Love walks on water, walks on coals, walks on air to put love into action. Moment by moment, love performs the impossible.

> *"Whoso loves, believes the impossible."*
> ***Elizabeth Barret Browning***

19

UNITE IN LOVE

Love loves celebrations because celebrations celebrate love.

We unite in love to celebrate our individual life passages—birthdays, anniversaries, graduations, promotions.

We unite in love to express our love for one another – Mother's Day, Father's Day, Valentine's Day, Secretary's Day, Grandparents Day, and so on.

We unite in love to share our cultural passages—independence days and cultural hero birthdays.

We unite in love to express our care of our planet home—Arbor Day and Earth Day.

We unite in love to honor our Spiritual Days, our Holy Days, and our Religious Days—too numerous to list.

Every day is a holiday many thousands of times over. Every day love is celebrating.

We can share in that. Every day we can think, "today is someone's birthday and I'm going to celebrate it all day long!" Every day we can be inside of love, filled with celebration.

> *"Every time we love,*
> *Every time we give,*
> *It's Christmas."*
> **Dale Evans**

20

LOVE LIKES EVERYBODY

An amazing aspect of love is that, along with loving everyone, it *likes* everyone. It doesn't put conditions and stipulations on your beliefs or my beliefs in order to be liked or loved. We all get to be precisely the flower we are meant to be, not criticized nor prejudiced against, whether growing in an orderly garden or coming up through a cracked sidewalk.

Love understands—better than we ourselves understand—our need to be just who we are in order to have the growth we are meant to have. How well it serves us when we learn from love's example.

Each of us can have our own ideas, ideals, knowledge, and relationship with the Divine, from our individual perspective, a perspective which is very different in an orderly garden with water, healthy soil, adequate sunshine, from that of a cracked sidewalk with virtually no water, nor nutrients, nor shade. How different thinking is likely to be in these disparate situations!

Yet love, ever and always, remains love, for all alike.

> *"We need not think alike
> to love alike."*
> **Francis David**

21

MORE LOVE, LESS PAPERWORK

It is strange and interesting how we can manifest so much distraction of our energies and our calling to make up other stuff—stuff that is just stuff.

What does that stuff have to do with the soul? What does it have to do with moving forward? What does it have to do with lighting the individual candles of the human family to add light to *all* our paths?

Ask love if you are on your purpose. Then be brave enough to listen to the answer. If one, or two, or all of your wheels are off your rails, ask love to help you get upon the tracks of your purpose. Love will find a way.

> *"What the world really needs*
> *Is more love and less paperwork."*
> **Pearl Bailey**

22

LOVE INSPIRES

One of the most lovable things about love is that when we feel it towards other people, other creatures, other processes, it inspires our love of self.

This is one way to learn and to know what your heart-mind-body sensations are teaching you.

People have often told me they're not sure what love is, or otherwise express what they call "love" in terms of possessiveness, selfishness, co-dependence, fear, abuse, and anger ... in the name of love, but sadly off the target.

Love, in one's heart-mind-body feels joyful, easy, rejuvenating and relaxed.

If we practice feeling joyful, easy, rejuvenated and relaxed towards others and towards the self every day, soon it no longer requires practice – it has become perfected!

> *"When we feel love and kindness toward others, it not only makes others feel loved and cared for, but (we) also develop inner happiness and peace."*
> **The Dalai Lama**

23

THE CIRCLE OF LOVE

The circle has always been a symbol of and for love - unbroken, with no beginning and no end. It's a symbol of Alpha and Omega, because that which has no beginning and no end contains within it, paradoxically, the energies of beginning and ending. Every ending is but a beginning.

We wear this symbol in rings of silver, gold, platinum, to signify eternity and the indestructibility of love.

> *"Come out of the circle of time*
> *And into the circle of love."*
> **Rumi**

24

TRUTH & LOVE

Truth and love are intimately related.

The further one is removed from the complete and total surrounding protection of love, the more not-truth is fostered. But we do not need—nor do we deserve!—to live outside of truth, outside of love.

Become disarmed in your relationship with truth, intimate and close in the same way that love relates to truth, and the last illusion separating you from love will melt, slip, fade away. When you love truth as love loves truth, you are brought into the inner sanctum of love, naturally and without hesitation.

> *"Unarmed truth and unconditional love will have the final word."*
> **Martin Luther King, Jr.**

25

LOVE PREVAILS

Trust in and know the Power of Love.

It can, does, and will break all swords, heal all ills, comfort all souls.

Fall back completely into the loving arms of love, with unabashed trust. Love will always catch you.

When things, desires, people and events all appear to abandon caring about you, love is always, always there.

Love will always prevail.

> *"When the power of love overcomes the love of power the world will know peace."*
> **Jimi Hendrix**

26

FAITH, HOPE, LOVE

We do not need any emotional agency other than that of love. There are many mansions in the domain of love, and all the other emotions we hold dear are within the loving care of love.

"Faith. Hope. Love.
The greatest of these is love."
1 Corinthians 13:13

27

LOVE'S HOME

Love holds all that is beautiful readily displayed for everyone to see. Only **LOOK!**

Love generously shares its dreams, its knowledge. Love knows there is no such thing as death, the grandest illusion of the three dimensions. But love does grant the illusion of death for the sake of getting our attention and getting us ignited to move forward with our lessons.

When taking an exam that passing or failing means we will pass or fail the entire class, we are motivated to study and apply ourselves during the exam.

Just so it is with life. If we don't hear the clock ticking, why be ardent in the pursuit of our lessons?

But love resides in eternity and pours out upon us many, many gifts and reinforcements as we apply ourselves to our lessons.

Beauty and creation's wonders abound and surround us.

"Love...
is the Morning and the Evening Star.
It is the mother of Art,
Love...
was the first to dream of immortality.
Love... fills the world with melody,
music is the voice of love.
Love is the magician
that changes worthless things to joy,
with (love), earth is heaven
and we are gods."
Robert G. Ingersoll

28

HONEY LOVE

Love makes all things sweet.

> *"Life is the flower for which love is the honey."*
> ***Victor Hugo***

29

ONLY BELIEVE IN LOVE

Those places that feel out of control, that appear volatile, mean-spirited, cruel, blinded by greed, avarice, destructiveness—they are as nothing to the power of love.

Love sweeps a beautiful hand over the landscape of unrest, terror, hardship, aggression, and all is healed.

Only believe in love. Belief in anger, terror, pain or abuse allows these illusions to perpetuate.

Belief in love brings love to the fore, and that is all there is!

> *"Love conquers all."*
> ***Virgil***

30

LOVE'S MIRACLES

Each of us has a story to tell about the miracles of love in our lives.

Many people hold these miracles as deeply kept, mystifying secrets. In my work with people, I've heard more than a few of these profound secrets.

At some point, such mystical experiences begin to accrue a critical mass that has a reality as real as our so-called reality.

These are not scary stories, although many people are frightened by their mystical experiences.

They are love stories.

*"Have you ever been at sea
in a dense fog, when it seemed
as if a tangible white darkness
shut you in and the great ship,
tense and anxious, groped her way
toward the shore with plummet
and sounding-line, and you waited
with beating heart
for something to happen?*

*"I was like that ship, only I was
without compass or sounding line,
and no way of knowing
how near the harbor was.*

*"Light! Give me light!"
was the wordless cry of my soul,
and the light of love shone on me
in that very hour!"*
Helen Keller

31

COMPASSION

There is an aspect of love that is the experience of feeling boundless, unconditional compassion. It is unlimited and without any nuance of prejudice.

That is to say, real, true compassion longs for and prays that all living beings, without exception, be free of suffering.

Compassion is not pity, which has about it a sense that one is glad it's not oneself who is suffering. True compassion empathizes with the sufferer and prays as if it is oneself, without, however, jumping down in the hole of suffering.

This is perhaps a strange-sounding, but a highly spiritual practice, to have a certain detachment from all suffering, one's own and that of others for the purpose of allowing the best solution or result to manifest.

The lesson of the highest level of love is not to wallow in suffering, which only calls more suffering to come into being. Love in the form of compassion asks us to understand that suffering is a transient state, and the more we imagine an image of not suffering, the sooner that picture will manifest.

To contemplate a concrete example, probably one of the strongest images that invokes compassion is that of starving children. If we react with pity ("oh that's terrible, those starving children. I'm glad they're not my children!"), this is not compassion. Pity is what Buddhism refers to as a "near enemy" of compassion.

If our reaction is a horrified aversion to the images of starving children, we feel overwhelmed and are not able to face it at all and turn away in a crippled state of pain. This is another "near enemy" to true compassion. The agency of sympathy is when we emotionally jump down in the hole with the pain and therefore are useless in assisting bringing about "not pain."

Only by responding (not reacting) with metta, agape love in the form of compassion can we begin to make a change, take action and envision effective means of eradicating suffering. There are amazing people doing miraculous work within the realm of compassion.

Ananada, Buddha's secretary, asked the Buddha, "Would it be true to say that the cultivation of loving kindness and compassion is a part of our practice?" To which the Buddha replied, "No. It would not be true to say that the cultivation of loving kindness and compassion is part of our practice. It would be true to say that the cultivation of loving kindness and compassion is *all* of our practice."

> "Compassion removes the suffering of others without expecting anything in return."
> **The Buddha**

32

COMPASSION FOR ONESELF

But before one can experience true compassion for others, one must first experience it for oneself. Again, not to pity yourself, which is a near enemy of compassion and is the status of being a victim. Victims call victimizers into their lives (and also become victimizers). All of which is outside of the realm of compassion.

> *"Compassion crushes and destroys the pain of others."*
> **The Buddha**

Do not be driven by aversion at any aspect of yourself – which is, as we more commonly call it, denial. Embrace that which is causing you to suffer. By this means are you healed.

Do not be cruel to yourself. How many times have you berated yourself, been judgmental about yourself, flogged yourself emotionally for what you deem an imperfection, for forgetting something, for failing a test, for a failed marriage, for being laid off, for all the hundreds of minor and major oversights, misunderstandings, poor communication, missed opportunities, etc., etc., that you've experienced in your life?

> *"Blessed are the merciful,*
> *For they shall obtain mercy."*
> **Matthew 5:7**

We are the harshest judges of ourselves and very much need unconditional compassion, the healing balm of love, patience and kindness poured out on ourselves first.

By this practice we learn the lessons of unconditional acceptance, compassion, and love, coming to the more complete, peace-filled, joy-radiating, love-and-compassion manifesting self.

When turning away from self-pity and aversion, you will discover the seemingly magical truth that you forget less, communicate better, and great opportunities often virtually land in your lap.

Love Yourself as You Would Have Others Love You

Nothing feels better than love. When love washes over us, whether it's for another person, a glorious sunrise, a bird singing in a tree, gratitude for some blessing or privilege or benefit that has befallen us, or simply love for oneself, we love it!

Everything we pursue is about the desire to experience the emotional and the bodily sensations of love. Love expands us.

> *"I feel good in a special way*
> *I'm in love and it's a sunny day."*
> **Paul McCartney, "Good Day Sunshine"**

33

AURA

Many people (including myself) see the light around living things. This light is the force of creation, it is the light of love.

If everyone opened the window in their mind that allows this vision, it would be, I hope, nearly impossible to experience hate for anyone. The profound reality of every single being having been created by the light of love would be inescapable.

Try it. Open the window in your mind that sees the light around every living thing. Love will pour in and through you as you have never, ever imagined.

> *"Everything around you is lovelight*
> *You're shining like a star in the night."*
> **Abba, "Lovelight"**

34

THE GATES OF HEAVEN

It's beautiful to picture that the Gates of Heaven are made of gigantic pearls, but more importantly, the Gates of Heaven are surely made of love, no matter where heaven may be, no matter whether internal or external, whether of physical form or of transdimensional form. One thing I know for sure—

Heaven is made of love.

And you hold the key to the Gates to Heaven.

> *"Love is the master key*
> *That opens the gates of happiness."*
> **Oliver Wendell Holmes**

35

THE FLOWER OF LOVE

How many kinds of love are there?
One.
How many forms does love take?
More than all the grains of sand that ever were or are or ever will be.
What makes love grow?
Nothing can stop it.

*"Love is the flower
You've got to let grow."*
John Lennon

36

LOVE HEALS ALL

Everyone has felt pain, everyone has felt abandoned, we all have wondered why the vagaries of life happen to us. We are good and kind.

And yet, bad things happen to us.

You've not been singled out, out of all the universe, to have sad and bad things happen to you. Challenges come upon every life.

You are being asked to remember one thing; LOVE.

Love will heal your wounds, cure your ills, and bring you back to the heart of love.

> *"One word frees us of all the weight and pain of life. That word is Love."*
> **Sophocles**

37

THE SPIRIT OF LOVE

Pretend you're from some other planet or dimension and you suddenly find yourself here, on earth.

Look around!

See the trees, the flowers, the rivers, the baby ducks and lambs, look at the moon, heavy in the western sky, the geese flying across it like a magic lantern show—as if you could reach out and touch it all.

Wouldn't you fall in love with this place?

Fall in love with every moment. Reside within the spirit of love.

> *"The moments you have truly lived are the moments you've done things in a spirit of love."*
> **Henry Drummond**

38

LOVE'S TRUE MEANS

Are you afraid?
 Discover safety in the world of love.
Are you sad?
 Be cheerful in the home of love.
Are you lonely?
 Meet friends at the party of love.

Are you restless?

Relax in the realm of love.

Are you bored?

Become active in the work of love.

Are you depressed?

Embrace joy in the halo of love.

Are you angry?

Experience laughter in the happiness of love.

Are you overwhelmed?

Release in the nap-time of love.

Are you judgmental?

Find kindness in the mind of love.

Are you lazy?

Energize in the field of love.

Are you self-critical?

Receive acceptance in the heart of love.

Are you codependent?

Meet your wonderful self in the mirror of love.

Are you less than truthful?

Learn the power of truth in the Wisdom School of love.

Are you feeling hopeless, helpless and lost?
Come into love in the arms of love.

> *"Love is the true means by which the world is enjoyed."*
> **Thomas Trahern**

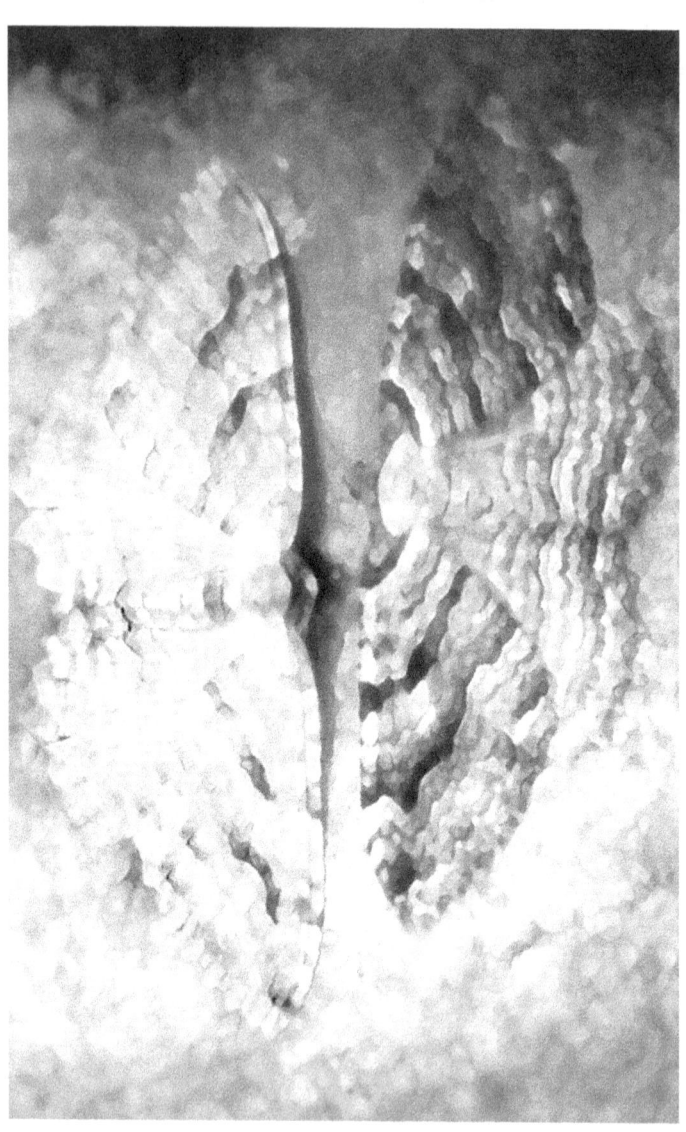

39

TIMELESS LOVE

Try this exercise the next time you're rushing to work, you're late to the airport, you're stuck in traffic, you're waiting for an appointment in a doctor's, dentist's, attorney's, CPA's office, you're in line at the grocery store, or any time you feel yourself under the oppression of time.

See yourself in a bubble of love. Picture that which you're hurrying to, or the person you're waiting for—imagine any and all in the bubble of love with you. You needn't concern yourself with time, because it is timeless inside of love.

You will usually discover that suddenly you're at work or on the airplane or your name is being called in a waiting room, or you're at the front of the check-out line.

When you place yourself in the domain of love and you focus on the timeless, you will learn that time becomes your servant instead of seeming to be master.

> *"Love is the emblem of eternity –*
> *It confounds all notion of time."*
> **Germaine DeStael**

40

REAL LOVE STORIES

Many of the emotions we've tagged "love" are actually forms of attachment, addiction, insecurity, loneliness or just plain control freaking energy. These, along with a host of other presentations of self, are turned aside from love.

One needn't be judgmental about these other emotional experiences. They are all teachers, and if we have in our mind a desire that all experiences bring us to love, then, eventually, they will. However, it's important, for one's centering and joy, to leave these emotions in their own clothing and not attempt to get them up in love's raiment.

You might, then, want to ask yourself: How may I experience and hold in my heart and mind, real love?

Here are some ways of looking at your emotions and your bodily feelings to receive answers to the foregoing question.

Do you feel jittery or uneasy when you are not with your love object (whether person, place, creature or thing)?

Do you feel anything resembling fear when you don't know exactly what the person of your attention is doing?

Do you find yourself giving the person or persons of your focus instructions and directives, unasked for because you know the best way to do things?

Answering truthfully yes to any of the foregoing questions is a beginning to acknowledging addiction, insecurity or control issues, emotions that are other than unconditional love. All of which may be "stations" at which we've stopped on the journey to love.

We are always empowered to get back on the train and move forward on our quest to true love.

The test of love is that it doesn't quit or stop. It continues and grows. Even if two people decide it does not serve each of their highest goals and purpose to continue to live together, they may physically separate, but they still love one another.

Enmity does not exist in unconditional love.

The people and the creatures we are learning to love, a journey which starts with yourself by the way, will all bask in the relaxing comfort of the love you radiate.

It will change your life in amazing and wonderful ways.

> *"Real love stories*
> *have no endings."*
> **Richard Bach**

ND
41

DARING TO LOVE

The most natural thing to do in this life is to love. But it's not always the easiest thing to do.

It takes courage to release our niggling wants and give them up to the power of love.

It takes a kind of stamina to focus on the larger goals in life, the ones that have as their underpinning unconditional love.

We dare to walk out on the tightrope of love, step by step, keeping our attention focussed on the balance where we are, and extending unconditional love to the goal we approach.

Sometimes it may feel like you are the only one up there on that high wire.

Guess what? It doesn't even matter if that's true – love will take care of you.

> *"The loving are the daring."*
> **Bayard Taylor**

42

MONEY CAN'T BUY ME LOVE

What would this world be like if people pursued love like they pursue money? Can you picture this? Millions and millions of people getting up in the morning, getting ready to leave home, getting in their cars or on public transportation to go to the office to nurture and produce love.

People spend their work days devising plans to feed everyone and making sure that every person, every family has a solid roof over their heads. Other people spend their work days figuring out ways to provide everyone who desires it an education, ways to get to schools and colleges, and getting them the books and supplies they need.

The people in the next office are organizing the housing, food, etc., for the folks who are taking care of education.

Artists and writers are producing their art from love and are provided homes and food and the tools of their trade.

Imagine our world fueled by love.

Just for a few moments, imagine it.

"I don't care too much for money,
Money can't buy me love."
Paul McCartney, "Can't Buy Me Love"

43

LOVE'S INSTINCT

There are many things that we know we know, even though we may not know *how* we know them.

The phone rings, you know it's Mother or your friend, Mary. Sure enough, even without caller ID, that's who's on the other end.

Perhaps you go to a job interview, and, although there are dozens of applicants, you know you are going to be offered the job. And you are offered the job.

Instinct is simply another word for love. True instinct has one purpose, one intention, and that is to serve you in the best way possible.

And so, too, it is of love.

> *"There is no instinct like that of the heart."*
> **Lord Byron**

44

THE BEST IN OTHERS

Everyone can be troublesome and trying at times – even thee and me. But love asks us to find the best in others.

This is occasionally tricky, but try this exercise to develop the habit. When you find yourself criticizing or being judgmental about someone, say, "but I hold that person in the light of unconditional love."

Maintain this thought until you feel a shift in yourself away from the judgmental energy, and you give yourself over to the flow of love.

How much more delicious and yummy is the feeling of love than the exhausting, dark energy of criticism! When you learn this, you'll rapidly discover that you'd much rather love than criticize.

You've moved from a lose-lose scenario where you feel crummy and you feel crummy about the other person, to a win-win, where you feel happy and you feel love for the challenging person. (It's also wise to remember that the things which we find difficult in another person are often reflecting some aspect of issues we're working on in ourselves.)

You may very likely see the challenging person, when on the receiving end of your unconditional love, moving towards being more lovable themselves.

> *"Find the best in others...*
> *Give of yourself...*
> *laugh often, and love much."*
> **Ralph Waldo Emerson**

45

THE WARP & WOOF OF LOVE

Try to contemplate this life, this world, this existence without love (which is a reach, because, again, everything has come into being through the agency of love). But, for a moment, pretend that everything is as it is, but there is no such thing as love.

There is nothing to look forward to when waking up in the morning.

One does not kiss one's beloved when leaving for work, because there is no love nor beloved.

You hear a bird song as you climb in the car, but you feel nothing because you have no love. In fact, you do not hear a bird song, because the bird is singing for the thrill of the sun arising, from the power of love, and there is none.

No buildings are built, no fields are planted, nothing is written. No art is painted, no drawings are drawn, no plays are staged, no songs are sung.

There is no pleasure in seeing beautiful children, no one goes to church, synagog, temple, mosque or meditation, no one is thankful for food, clothes, shelter, no one has a picnic, no one laughs or lends a helping hand. No one stands in awe where the ocean meets the shore.

The warp and woof of our lives are inspired by love.

Listen, with all your heart, to every bird song!

"Without love I am nothing."
I Corinthians 14:9

46

LOVE CONQUERS ALL

It doesn't get any more simple than this—there is nothing love cannot conquer.

> "There is no difficulty that love will not conquer,
> No disease that love will not heal,
> No door that love will not open,
> No gulf that love will not bridge,

*No wall that love will not throw down,
No sin that love will not redeem."*
Emmet Fox

47

LISTEN FOR LOVE'S VOICE

Is there anything we need to know, or feel, or sense, beyond love? Love will answer every question. If you have been asking, but it does not seem that love responds, begin, then, to **LISTEN**!

> "Whatever the question,
> Love is the answer."
> **Anonymous**

48

LOVE'S TENACITY

I took this photograph in Central America at a step pyramid site. As much as I was fascinated by the cultural artifacts there, this valiant little tree, coming out of an ancient wall twenty feet up from the ground, arrested my attention. It immediately came to mind as a glorious tribute to, and metaphor for, love.

Love will not be dissuaded. Love will not be hampered. Love will find its way, will grow in any soil, or minimal soil or virtually no soil.

All we need is the thought of love, and it manifests, grows, and becomes a beautiful, living process.

Never doubt the presence or the power of love. No matter how tightly constructed anyone's walls may be, love will grow there.

Rejoice!

49

AMAZING LOVE

Love is lovely wherever we encounter it. But the truest test of love is not between kingdoms or nations or tribes.

The sweetest look at love is not in grand undertakings.

The most amazing unfolding of the experience of love is between two people who weathered together all of life's storms, pains, and battles, who have cherished one another.

Who have fought, argued, disagreed, cried, felt lonely, and hurt.

Who have apologized, made up, come to an agreement, or agreed to disagree, laughed, been companioned, and healed.

Who have forgiven times multiplied by times, who have been there for one another as the sun arises and who have returned to the same hut in the woods as the long rays of sunset stretch out shadows across the land.

Love's triumph is in two people who still watch the stars together after many, many years and who say from their hearts ....

"I'd still rather watch the stars with you," whether those stars are in the sky or in each other's eyes.

*"Love at first sight
is easy to understand;
it's when two people
have been looking at each other
for a lifetime that love
becomes a miracle."*
Amy Bloom

*"That Love is all there is,
Is all we know of Love."*

Emily Dickinson

Dear Reader ....

I hope you discovered some meaningful insights when reading *Love is the Answer*. If you would like a free copy of the ebook: *Horn of Plenty – The Cornucopia of Your Life*, send your request to me at:

Blythe@BlytheAyne.com

About the Author

I live in a forest with a few domestic and numerous wild creatures, where I create an ever-growing inventory of books, both nonfiction and fiction, short stories, illustrated kid's books, and articles, with a bit of wood carving when I need a change of pace.

I received my Doctorate from the University of California at Irvine in the School of Social Sciences, majoring in psychology and ethnography, after which I moved to the Pacific Northwest to write and to have a modest private psychotherapy practice in a small town not much bigger than a village.

Finally I decided it was time to put my full focus on my writing, where, through the world-shrinking internet, I could "meet" greater numbers of people. Where I could meet you!

If **Love is the Answer** has touched you in a positive way I hope you'll consider writing a review, as reviews are an excellent means for other people to discover books that inspire them on their way.

I Wish You Happiness, Health, Peace, and Joy,
Blythe

Questions, comments? I'd love to hear from you!:

Blythe@BlytheAyne.com

www.BlytheAyne.com

www.ingramcontent.com/pod-product-compliance
Lightning Source LLC
Chambersburg PA
CBHW071738080526
44588CB00013B/2082